THE SPIRIT OF THE LABYRINTH

THE SPIRIT OF THE LABYRINTH

A True Tail of Love

Eve Eschner Hogan, MA

Copyright © 2019, 2022 by Eve Eschner Hogan.

All rights reserved.
First edition 2019
Second edition 2022

No part of this book may be reproduced or transmitted in any form or by any means whatsoever, including graphic, electronic, or mechanical, including photocopying, recording, taping, or by any information storage or retrieval system, without permission from the publisher.

Printed in the United States of America

Cover and interior design and layout by Constellation Book Services

Image on page 77 reproduced by kind permission of jacquielawson.com

ISBN-13: 978-1-888973-02-0 (print)
ISBN-13: 978-1-888973-03-7 (ebook)

Dedicated to Steve Hogan.

For sharing the love, the emotion, and the magic with me—and our furry and feathery family.

One day an angel walked into our nursery and peace sanctuary, The Sacred Garden, on the beautiful island of Maui. This angel was extraordinarily large and exceptionally hot.

Rather than the light feathers we might think of when we think of angels, she was wearing a big white and brown, heavy, fur coat because…she was a Saint Bernard dog named Angel! In the warmth and humidity of the tropics, this angel was miserable!

She quickly looked around and searched for places to cool off. She tried the shade under the plant benches, but she was still too hot. She looked around some more and that is when she saw it! A koi pond! It was the perfect sized bathtub for her overheated body.

Much to the surprise of the koi who called the pond their home, Angel climbed right in sending them scattering to the edges to get away from this very unusual visitor to their otherwise uneventful pond.

Ah....Much Better!

As the owner of The Sacred Garden, I laughed while observing Angel in the fish pond and innocently said, "I always wanted a St. Bernard when I was a little girl," fondly remembering the huge dog I walked past in my neighborhood over forty years ago.

Angel's guardian person said, "She's pregnant! I'll call you when the puppies are born."

I smiled politely knowing full well that neither my husband, Steve, nor I were interested in another pet. I bid them farewell and promptly forgot all about the puppies.

A couple of months later, Angel's guardian person called saying, "The puppies were born, and are ready for adoption!"

I gently explained that I wasn't looking to adopt. Angel's person said, "That's okay. Just come see them; they are super cute!"

Knowing all too well that "just seeing a puppy" is the number one way to WANT a puppy, I politely declined.

Later that day, I mentioned the puppies to Steve, who exclaimed with conviction, "No! Don't go see the puppies!!!!" He also knew exactly what would happen if their magic love spell fell on me. So I did not go and again forgot all about the puppies.

A few days later, into The Sacred Garden walked Angel, her guardian person, and a bunch of the cutest, biggest puppies you have ever seen! Now most puppies fit in the palms of your hands at nine weeks old, but these Saint Weiler puppies (half Saint Bernard, half Rottweiler) were already 20 pounds!

Did I mention cute?

They were unreasonably CUTE!

One of the puppies, the biggest of them, turned his head and his big brown eyes looked into mine and it was all over. I was instantly in love with him. The other puppies were adorable too, but this one was extra special. The magic love spell did its job; I wanted to keep him.

But what was I to do about Steve who had clearly said NO to a pup?

I called him up and sweetly said, "Hey Honey, the puppies are in the garden."

To which Steve predictably replied, "No puppies."

I said, "I know, I know, *just come see them*!"

The minute Steve saw the puppies the same magic spell was cast over him, but he tried hard to resist. I looked at him pleadingly.

Steve said, "Do you know how BIG this puppy is going to get?"

Angel was 155 pounds and the Rottweiler father was similarly large. I nodded (not *really* knowing *exactly* how big BIG was.) As Steve struggled between his logic and the love spell, he finally suggested that I consider the smaller, girl puppy.

With the boy puppy in my arms, I continued to look at Steve for consent. Finally, he gave in saying, "Do whatever you want."

I laughed, "If I can do whatever I want I will take this boy AND his little sister!"

Steve quickly chimed in, "No, only one! We can have *one*!"

And there it was — permission granted!

The beautiful bouncing baby puppy had found a loving home and instantly became a huge part our family, of The Sacred Garden —and of our hearts.

The next task was to name the puppy.

I thought and thought about this. Since there are two labyrinths at The Sacred Garden and minotaurs and labyrinths go together in Greek Mythology, I thought it would be funny to name him Minotaur.

But then, considering the power and the energy of a name, and the recognition that minotaurs are known to eat young men and women in the center of the labyrinth as a sacrifice, I thought that was perhaps a bad idea.

And, calling him "Mini" for short, didn't make a lot of sense either.

I thought about Bear, because he certainly looked like a bear cub, but again, not the gentlest of animals to dwell in a peaceful garden.

I sat in front of the beautiful, large Buddha in the garden meditating on a name for the pup, when "Bodhi" popped into my head. The Buddha had sat under a Bodhi tree and Bodhi meant Enlightened or Awakened— possessing an understanding of the true divine nature of all things.

Bodhi was the perfect name for this (mostly) gentle being.

A Bodhisattva: an enlightened one.

Bodhi set out to explore his new world and got into a little mischief.
He thought it was funny to pretend he had been run over...

He found a water bowl but had to stand on his "tippy paws" to drink out of it —

for now.

The next step was to grow. And grow he did. Bodhi put on half a pound a day for nearly an entire year!

See the angel on his chest?

That is his "mom" tattoo!

At eighteen months he thought he was still a lap dog!

He eventually reached 175 pounds!

Quite frankly, he was HUGE!

And so were his paws!

And so was his nose!

He no longer had to stand on his "tippy paws" to drink from the giant water bowl.

He became my guardian dog, and when I was in The Sacred Garden or in the yard, Bodhi was with me.

Just like his mom, Bodhi also liked to cool off in water, but the garden's koi fish were happy he used the stream in the back yard instead of climbing into their pond!

We all know dogs love to go for walks.

In fact, most of us can't even say the word, "Walk" without putting our pups into a high level of excitement. We carefully spell the word out, "W-A-L-K" thinking that they don't know how to spell, only to discover they quickly figure out what that strange way of saying WALK means!

Bodhi was no exception.

And boy was he in the right place.

The Sacred Garden hosts labyrinth WALKS. These circuitous journeys are intended for the walkers to reach the sacred center, symbolic of one's own sacred center, where they can experience God.

Bodhi, however, got this a little backwards and decided that the labyrinth WALK was where people should experience DOG!

He loved the labyrinth.
He joined every labyrinth walk he could.

Every time I walked the labyrinth, he would make his way to the center and wait for me there.

Bodhi realized that rather than being a pilgrim journeying to and from a sacred destination, he could stay at the destination and watch the pilgrims come and go.

He quickly discovered that if he just went to the center of the labyrinth and waited patiently, all the pilgrims would eventually find him there—and delightedly so.

He knew where the LOVE was found.

Like a kinder, gentler version of a Minotaur, he would greet them in the center and they showered him with love—and vice versa.

He happily ate it up.

He just seemed to know that people needed some companionship when they reached the center, to know they were not alone, that love was right there waiting for them all along.

His strength was empowering.

His presence was healing.

His sweetness was a good reminder; a god reminder.

His stillness was a good reminder, too.

He even showed us that sometimes our obstacles on the journey just need a little of our attention.

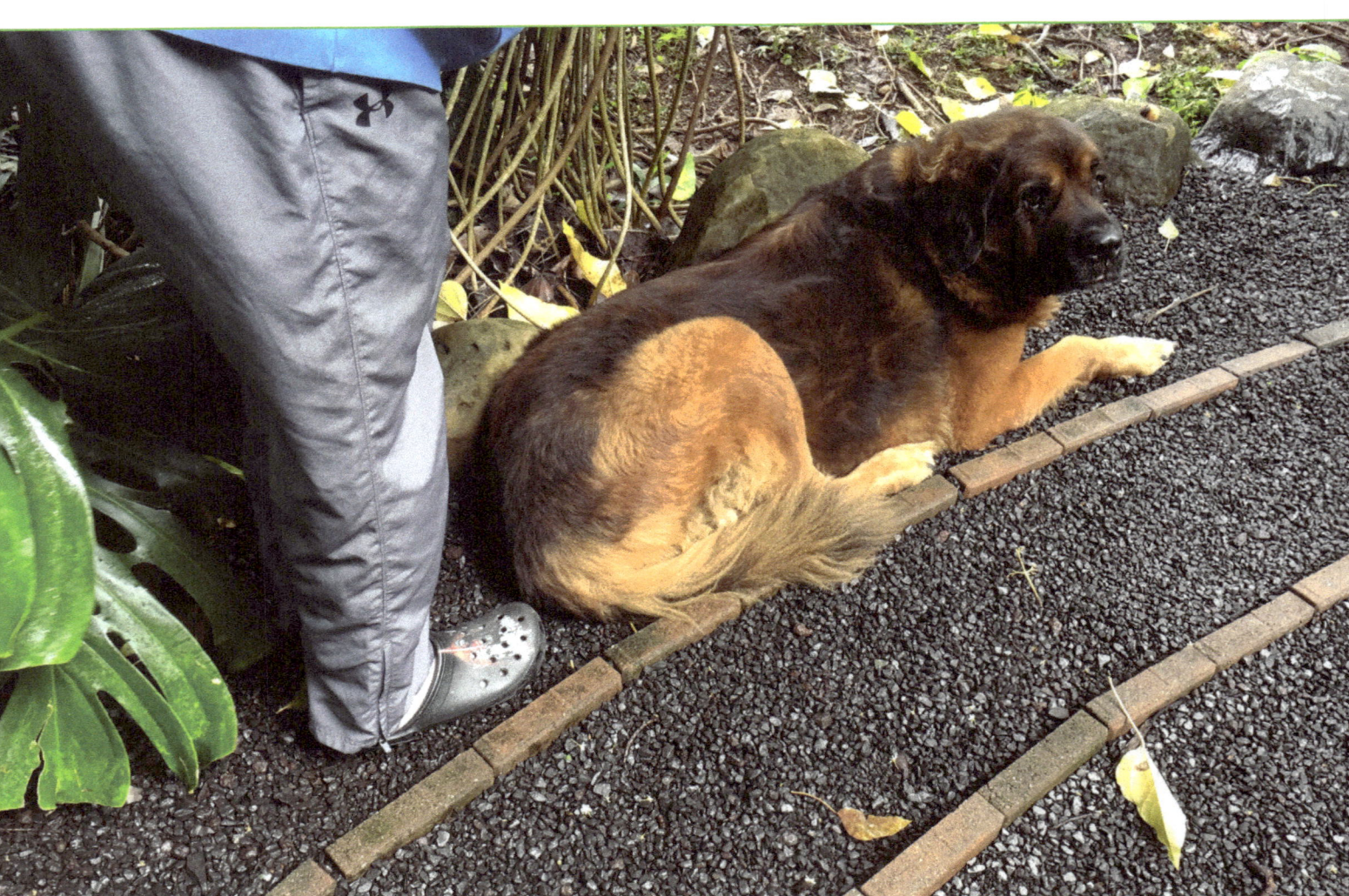

He had a special way of comforting.

Sometimes I would find him sitting in the center all by himself, taunting passers-by, suggesting they, too, join him in the sacred circle.

Everybody loved Bodhi. Well, except the people who were scared to death of his mere size. So, let's say everybody who wasn't scared of Bodhi loved him.

He soon became **The Sacred Garden mascot**. People would come specifically to see the gentle giant, and to walk the labyrinth with him or pose for pictures.

He loved to join wedding photo shoots.

Photo Credit Greg Hoxie

He attended tea ceremonies.

He met monks.

He joined the meditation circles.

He joined the Quaker's circle.

He joined in private meditations.

And he meditated on his own.

He even made it into paintings.

Painting by Louie Carone

Art by Andrea Scott

Painting by Wide Garcia

And Sunset Magazine!

But he always returned from his adventures to the center of the labyrinth—every one he could find.

Jesus Painting by Bruce Harman

Bodhi joined us for every monthly full moon labyrinth walk. He patiently sat in front of the Buddha while I gave the talk, then went outside for his favorite part: THE WALK.

He went straight to the center and waited for the love to come and go.

Labyrinth walks and Bodhi went paw in paw.

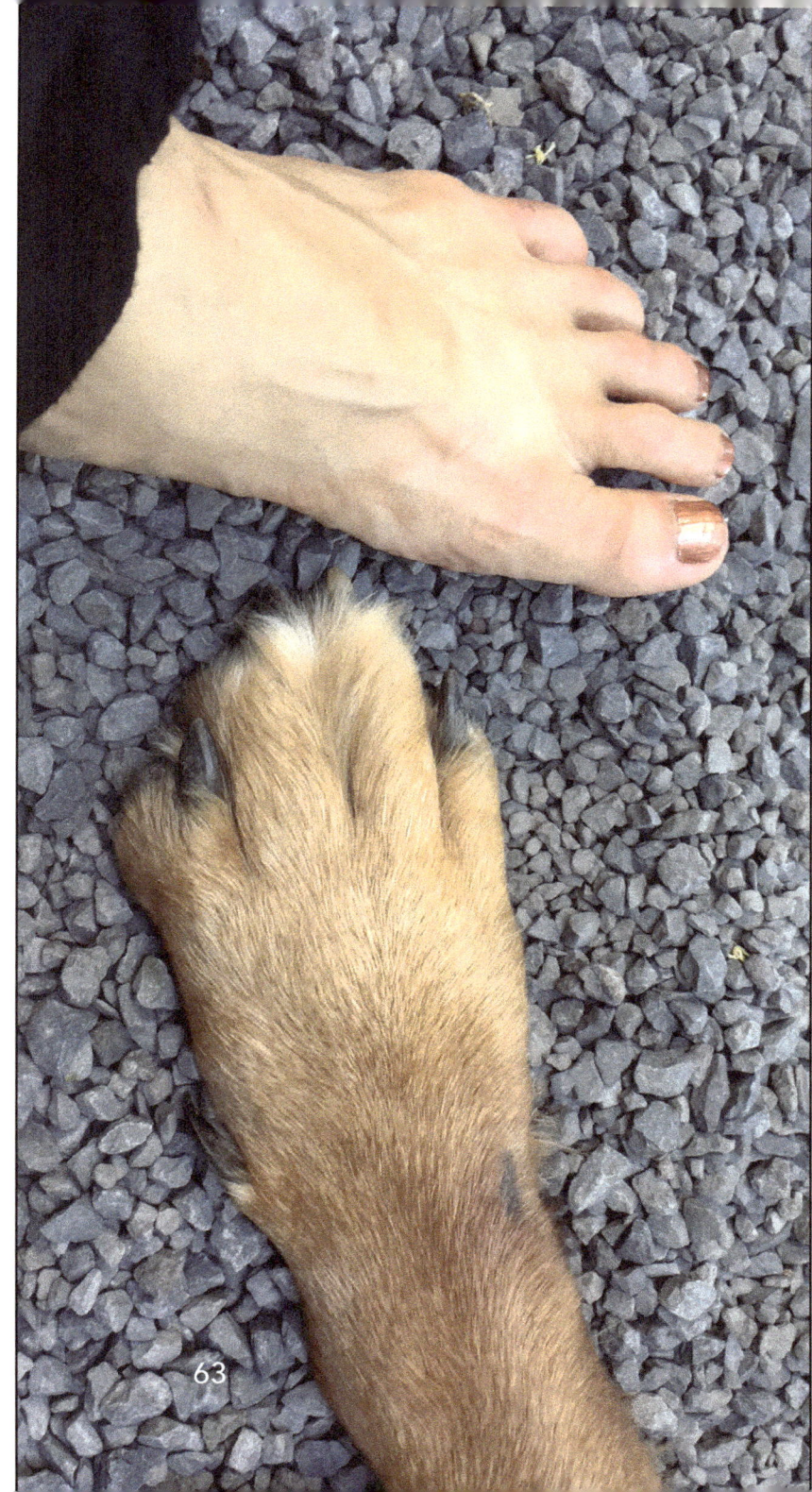

Then one day, Bodhi started to limp. Thinking he had just a minor injury, we kept an eye on him. But over the next few days it seemed to get worse instead of better and a lump developed on his leg, so I took him to the veterinarian.

I could see the sadness in the veterinarian's eyes and knew that it wasn't good news. He told me Bodhi had very fast growing bone cancer and that there was nothing they could do about it. They gave me pain medication for him and told me to take him home and love him up—in preparation to say good-bye.

My questions turned from, Was he in pain? How long would it take? to:

What was I going to do without my spirit animal, my companion, my Bodhisattva?

What would The Sacred Garden be without Bodhi, our mascot?

What would Steve do without his "explore the river" dog and our protector?

Bodhi got weaker and weaker by the day and we had the very difficult decision of what to do. If we let the cancer take its course, Bodhi would be in a lot of pain, and he risked breaking his leg where the bone tumor made it weak. But we couldn't stand the thought of losing him.

Then the day came, just three weeks after we got the news, when he could barely stand or walk and he was clearly in more pain than the medicine could handle.

We sadly faced the reality that if we didn't have the veterinarian come and put him out of his misery, he could shatter his leg in any given moment. We didn't want his last experience in this magnificent body, in this magnificent life, to be full of pain and stress. We wanted his last moments to be calm and loving. So we made an appointment for the next morning for the veterinarian to come to our house at The Sacred Garden.

That morning I got up early and loved Bodhi up. I explained to him what was happening and told him to find me again, when he was ready to reincarnate. I figured that he was like the Dalai Lama who would find another body, be reborn and return to me again. So, I asked him to give me a sign so I would know a new puppy was him.

I thanked him for all the love,
the protection and the company.

He held my hand to comfort me and
I held his paw to comfort him.

Then, I got a gigantic jar of peanut butter from the house (because that was one of Bodhi's favorite treats)! Rather than the normal allotment of one or two spoonfuls, I gave him the entire jar, a handful at a time.

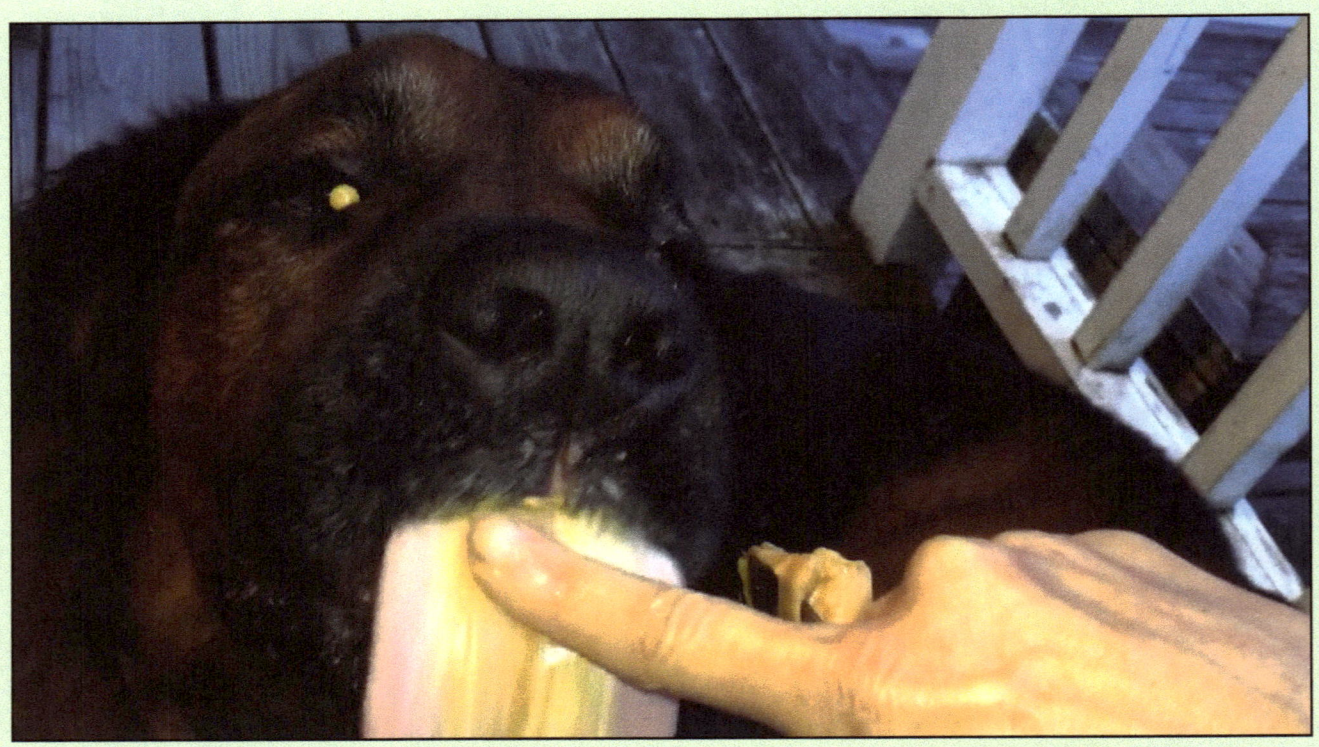

And, along with the love, he ate it up.

When he was done, he got up and started to walk toward the stairs leading from my front porch down to the yard. I almost stopped him because I was scared he would break his leg going down the stairs. But then, I decided that since the veterinarian was on her way over, I would let him go where he wanted to go.

He carefully hobbled his way down the stairs and started walking through the yard with me following right behind him, wondering where he was going.

He turned and walked alongside The Sacred Garden nursery, then turned left.

And went straight for the center of the labyrinth, his favorite, special place.

He laid down in the center, and Steve and I joined him there.

I put my "paw" on his heart to comfort him.

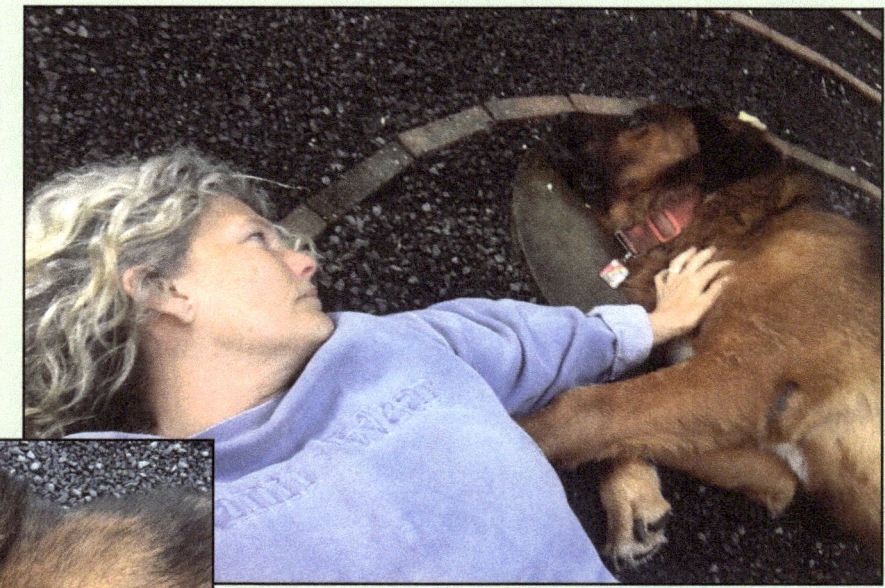

And he put his "hand" on my knee to comfort me.

We shared silence, sobs and love until the veterinarian came.

Bodhi passed away peacefully in his favorite place, the center of the labyrinth.

He was 107 months old to the day.

In the month that followed everyone around the garden was feeling the loss of our beautiful mascot.

Complete strangers to me, but beloved friends of Bodhi's, would come into the garden crying. People sent cards, pictures, flowers and heartfelt prayers.

It was clear that Bodhi had touched many people's hearts as the official garden greeter.

One day, when the pain and loss was just too hard to handle, Steve and I began a gentle search for a new puppy.

I didn't just want ANY puppy; I wanted Bodhi in his new body—which made the search a little tougher.

There were several extremely cute puppies available, but they had all been born before Bodhi died, and I wanted to at least give Bodhi's spirit a chance to find a new puppy body.

Finally, a litter of Golden Retriever puppies was posted, born 28 days after Bodhi's death and three days before, what would have been, his 108 month birthday.

We contacted the caretakers, met with them and put down a deposit. Eventually, we would get second pick of the litter, but for now we couldn't even see the puppies.

They understandably wanted the momma dog to adjust to parenting in privacy.

We went home to wait but, instead of being excited, I went into an emotional funk. I lamented to Steve that I felt like I had betrayed my agreement with Bodhi. I had by-passed the "magic." I hadn't even looked into the puppy's eyes to see that it was Bodhi. I hadn't waited for the sign I had asked him to send me.

Steve assured me the new puppy would be wonderful, and I was sure he was right. But, I didn't want just *any* puppy. I wanted the one with the big brown eyes.

The next morning I woke up thinking about the puppy and, still lying in bed, had a heart to heart talk with Bodhi's spirit. I told him about the puppy and how I hoped that he was in that litter. I told him that when I got to see the puppies, I would look for his eyes....

Then I checked my email.

First, there was a "Happy Birthday Bodhi" email from the veterinarian. Ah yes, this was Bodhi's birthday. I closed my eyes and sent him extra love as another wave of grief passed over me.

Then, I opened my eyes and returned to my email. And the next email said, "Canine Conjuring Tricks—and a balloon…"

CANINE CONJURING TRICKS???!!!

Not only had I never gotten an email with a subject like that but I'd never even seen the phrase in any context ever before. But, a canine conjuring trick was EXACTLY what I needed!

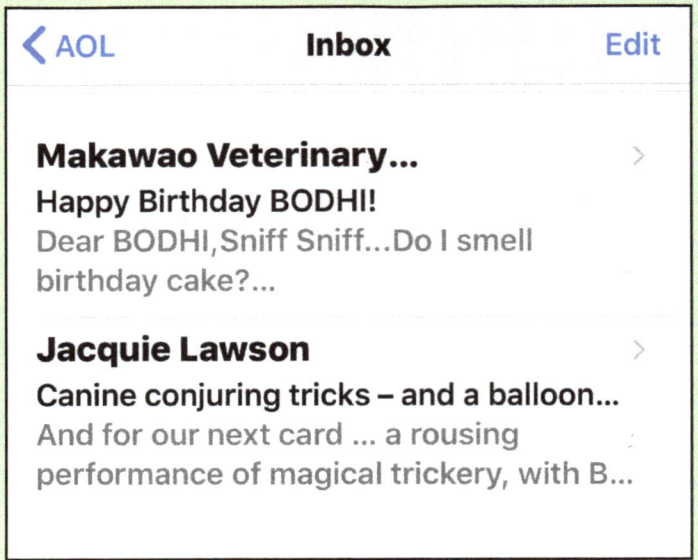

I opened the email excitedly and it was a Jacquie Lawson BIRTHDAY CARD with a picture of a GOLDEN RETRIEVER dog with a MAGIC WAND in its mouth and a birthday cake—on Bodhi's birthday!

Still curious as to exactly what a canine conjuring trick might be, I clicked on the link to the card and an animated bunny jumped into a hat. The Golden Retriever tapped the hat with a MAGIC WAND and turned the bunny into a PUPPY!

Now, you can call all that coincidental, but I think a birthday card on Bodhi's birthday of a GOLDEN RETRIEVER with a MAGIC WAND making a PUPPY is a pretty clear MAGICAL SIGN... that a puppy has been conjured up!

NOW I was excited!

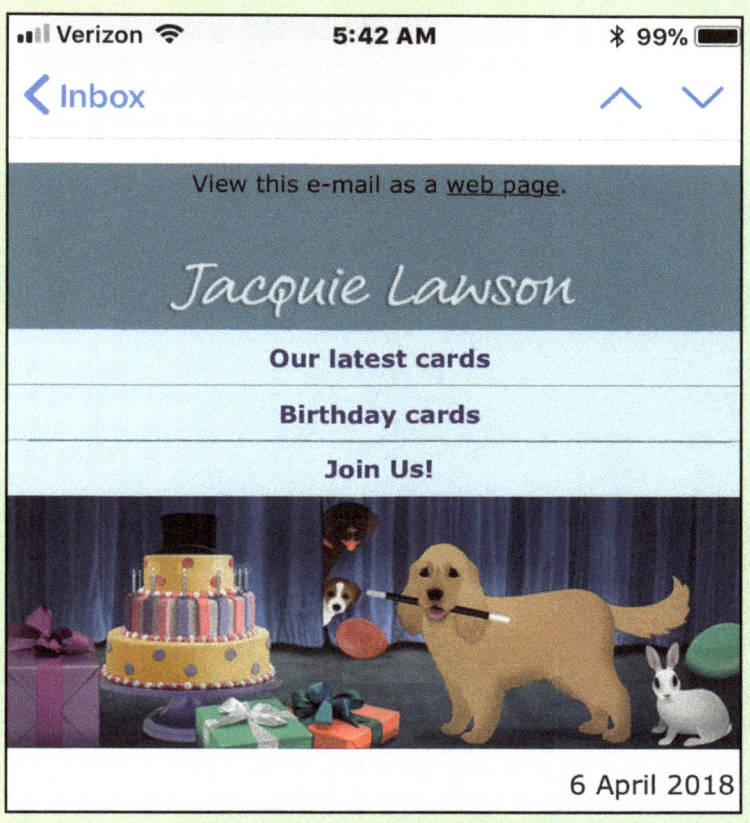

And then the day finally came when the pups were old enough for us to meet them. I wondered if I would really be able to tell which one was Bodhi.

Would he come back as a boy, or a girl? Would I know him when I saw him (or her)?

All of the puppies were adorable and really, they all looked pretty much the same. But while all the other puppies were busy being puppies, one of the puppies, the biggest of them, turned its head and its big brown eyes looked into mine. It was all over. The magic love spell was cast and right then, I knew.

Can you tell which one?

It was love at first sight.
But this time, the big brown eyes belonged to a precious little girl!

The next task was to name the puppy.

Again we thought and thought and thought about this. Steve would come up with a name that I didn't like, and I would come up with a name that he didn't like.

Then, we finally found one that worked for both of us (that is how you know it is right).

We named the new puppy "Kumu" which means "teacher" in Hawaiian.

If there is anything we knew for sure, it was that Kumu, just like Bodhi, would teach us about unconditional, eternal love—that is bigger than bodies (even big bodies)!

**So we brought Kumu home
and she taught us to begin again.**

The Sacred Garden has a new mascot.
I have another guardian watching over me.
Steve has a new companion to go exploring with by the stream.
Visitors have a new opportunity to share love and pose for pictures.
There is a new presence joining the meditation circles.

And, a teacher can be found in the center of the labyrinth reminding us of the true divine nature of all beings, and that love never dies.

This journey leads us round and round,
through twists and turns,
love lost and found,
always to the center, our center,
where the Spirit of the Labyrinth dwells.

**Sometimes in the form of God;
Sometimes in the form of Dog.**

The End …???

ABOUT THE AUTHOR
Eve Eschner Hogan

Photo Credit: Greg Hoxsie

 Eve is a labyrinth facilitator and the owner of The Sacred Garden on Maui—a peaceful destination, home of two labyrinths and a beautiful nursery which are free to the public and open daily. She is also the owner of Heart Path Journeys, offering personalized retreats and presentations, and is a wedding officiant. Eve is the author of several books including, *The EROS Equation: A Soul-ution for Relationships*, and *Way of the Winding Path: A Map for the Labyrinth of Life*.

For more information: EveHogan.com, SacredMauiRetreats.com, SacredGardenMaui.com, and SacredGardenRetreat.com

LABYRINTHS AT THE SACRED GARDEN

The Sacred Garden offers two different styles of labyrinths, a seven-circuit and an eleven-circuit, which serve as contemplative paths. The "circuits" are the number of times the single path passes between the outside and the center of the labyrinth. Some walk them for fun, others for self-discovery and personal awareness, others to process grief, or as a path of problem resolution, while others use it as a walking meditation or path of prayer.

Some helpful things to know:

- The labyrinth is not a maze, there is just one path that leads into the center and the same path leads back out.
- You are not walking the labyrinth to learn about the labyrinth, but rather, you are walking to learn about yourself.
- The "language of the labyrinth" is metaphor, meaning that everything you notice and everything you experience on the labyrinth is mirroring something you are invited to look at in yourself.

  For example, if you are judgmental on the labyrinth or full of self-doubt, the labyrinth offers you an opportunity to set yourself free of those behaviors—if even for just a few minutes. See what happens when you stop trying to control that which you have no control over and when you practice acceptance of yourself and others.

- The labyrinth is a beautiful tool for self-discovery, and an opportunity to practice bringing your words, thoughts and actions into alignment with your highest (and healthiest) self.

ELEVEN-CIRCUIT LABYRINTH

The labyrinth nestled in a beautiful Kukui tree grove beside Maliko Stream is a replica of the labyrinth found in the floor of the Chartres Cathedral in France, dating back to 1200 CE. It was part of the spiritual tradition of the time to take a pilgrimage to places like Jerusalem but the Crusades made the journey dangerous. It is believed they built the labyrinth within the safety of the church so people could walk a symbolic pilgrimage, with the center of the labyrinth representing the sacred destination.

SEVEN-CIRCUIT LABYRINTH

Inside The Sacred Garden greenhouse, sitting below a beautiful painting of Jesus, is a much older style labyrinth known as a "Classic or Universal Labyrinth." This simpler pattern dates back 4,000-5,000 years and was found all over the world (Greece, India, Scandinavia, Italy, Native American tradition) and no one knows how they all got the same design.

www.ingramcontent.com/pod-product-compliance
Lightning Source LLC
Chambersburg PA
CBHW041218240426
43661CB00012B/1077